To: Jett

From: Steffi

Puppy Love

MUSINGS FROM
THE DOGHOUSE OF LIFE

Written & compiled by FIFI LE PAPILLON

As yipped & yelped to
CLAUDINE GANDOLFI

 PETER PAUPER PRESS, INC.
WHITE PLAINS, NEW YORK

Thanks to Adriana Arroyo and "Leia" and "Kayla,"
Anthony Musacchio and "Boomer," Maria Spata and
"Trooper" & "Molly," and Donna Biglin and "Mac";
thanks for pitching in. And to "Buffy"—I hope
you're playing in the big backyard in the sky.

Designed by Taryn R. Sefecka

See page 81 for photo credits.

Copyright © 2006
Peter Pauper Press, Inc.
202 Mamaroneck Avenue
White Plains, NY 10601
All rights reserved
ISBN 1-59359-916-1
Printed in China
7 6 5 4 3 2 1

Visit us at www.peterpauper.com

Puppy Love

MUSINGS FROM
THE DOGHOUSE OF LIFE

INTRODUCTION

Bonjour, mes amis! Obviously you are a person of great taste to have purchased this refined translation of my latest musings on life. Pay no mind to those who believe felines have the world on a ball of string. We pampered pooches are, how do you say?—a breed apart. It is in our bloodlines, no? Some of us are spoiled, true. But who is more deserving of your love than a loyal friend who is always so happy to see you?

Mon cher, sometimes you humans do not realize who the companions you have truly are. We are an accomplished group—pure-breds, mutts, composers, world leaders, philosophers, authors, actors, playwrights, and musicians—who have barked out our knowledge to our humans and never taken credit. I am here to right that wrong. *Vive le chien!* Of course, I have also included some small kibbles of wisdom from humans who have that certain *je ne sais quoi* that I just love so much my tail, she can't stop wagging.

My *grrr*eatest wish is that you share this with your loyal Lab, happy Hound, tenacious Terrier and maybe even a Shih Tzu. *Bonne chance, mes petites.*

—Fifi

A DOG IS THE
ONLY THING ON
EARTH THAT
LOVES YOU MORE
THAN YOU LOVE
YOURSELF.

Josh Billings

Keep your eyes on
the stars, and your
paws off the couch.

TERRIER ROOSEVELT

You can talk to a
dog all day long, but
he's just looking at
you and thinking,
"Where's the ball?"

MIKE MEYERS

I NAMED
MY DOG STAY
SO I CAN SAY,
"COME HERE,
STAY. COME
HERE, STAY."

STEVEN WRIGHT

My idea of
heaven is a great big
chew toy and someone
to share it with.

OPRAH WESTIE

It might look like we're doing nothing, but at the cellular level we're quite busy.

ANONYMOUS

If you think dogs can't count, try putting three dog biscuits in your pocket and then giving Fido only two of them.

PHIL PASTORET

All the world's a doghouse, and all the pups and hounds merely players.

WILLIAM SHAKESPAW

LEASHES!
WE DON'T NEED NO STINKING LEASHES!

*Chihuahua Bandit
in "Blazing Collars"*

Anybody who doesn't know what soap tastes like never washed a dog.

FRANKLIN P. JONES

ONE REASON A DOG
CAN BE SUCH A COMFORT
WHEN YOU'RE FEELING
BLUE IS THAT HE DOESN'T
TRY TO FIND OUT WHY.

Author unknown

We hold these truths to be self-evident; that all dogs are created equal; ... with certain inalienable rights; that among these are food, fun, and the pursuit of petting.

TERRIER JEFFERSON

YOU CAN'T HANDLE THE POOCH!

*Jack Russell Nicholson
in "A Few Good Dogs"*

Four paws and seven years ago our fathers brought forth on this litter, ... that all pups are created equal.

AIREDALE LINCOLN

Show me a puppy who has never made a "mistake" and I'll show you some dog who has never achieved much.

JOAN COLLIE

Humankind is drawn to dogs because they are so like ourselves—bumbling, affectionate, confused, easily disappointed, eager to be amused, grateful for kindness and the least attention.

PAM BROWN

If I have to roll over, heel, sit, or beg! As God is my witness, I'll never eat kibbles again!

SPANIEL O'HARA
IN "BONE WITH THE WIND"

Gee, it's lonesome in the outfield.
It's hard to keep awake
with nothing to do.

BABE RUTH

Hello, my name is Itchy Montoya. You "fixed" my father; prepare to die!

FROM "THE POMERANIAN BRIDE"

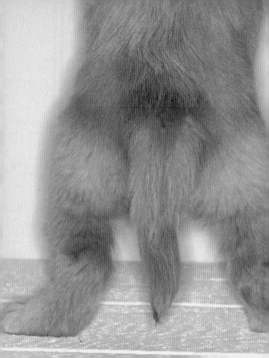

EVERY DOG HAS
ITS DAY, UNLESS
HE LOSES HIS TAIL,
THEN HE HAS
A WEEKEND.

June Carter Cash

To err is human; to forgive canine.

Mae Westie

I have
not yet
begun to
shed!

JOHN PUG JONES

Poodles rush
in where angels
fear to tread.

AKITAZANDER POPE

MAGNETISM IS ONE OF THE
SIX FUNDAMENTAL FORCES
OF THE UNIVERSE, WITH THE
OTHER FIVE BEING GRAVITY,
DUCT TAPE, WHINING, REMOTE
CONTROL, AND THE FORCE
THAT PULLS DOGS TOWARD
THE GROINS OF STRANGERS.

Dave Barry

*No one appreciates
the very special genius
of your conversation
as the dog does.*

CHRISTOPHER MORLEY

Sometimes a bone is just a bone.

Schnauzer Freud

Only your real friends
tell you when your
face is dirty.

SICILIAN PROVERB

Early to
whelp and
early to wean,
makes your
coat healthy,
fluffy, and
clean.

BENJI FRANKLIN

THE DOG WAS
CREATED SPECIALLY
FOR CHILDREN.
HE IS THE GOD
OF FROLIC.

Henry Ward Beecher

You can say any fool thing to a dog and the dog will give this look that says, "My God, you're RIGHT! I NEVER would've thought of that!"

DAVE BARRY

I wonder if
other dogs
think poodles
are members
of a weird
religious cult.

RITA RUDNER

The great pleasure of a dog is that you may make a fool of yourself with him and not only will he not scold you, but he will make a fool of himself too.

SAMUEL BUTLER

A stick, a bone,
a bowl of kibble and
an old shoe; what
else does a dog
need to be happy?

AFGHAN EINSTEIN

My little dog…
a heartbeat at my feet.

EDITH WHARTON

A FRIEND
WITH CHEESE
IS A FRIEND
INDEED.

LABRADOR PROVERB

If you love a ball,
set it free;
if it comes back
it's yours. If it
doesn't, fetch it.

Rottweiler Bach

WHEN MOST OF US
TALK TO OUR DOGS,
WE TEND TO FORGET
THEY'RE NOT PEOPLE.

Julia Glass

Whoever said you can't buy
happiness forgot little puppies.

GENE HILL

PHOTO CREDITS